PLAYING THE CELLO

an approach through live music making

by Hugo Cole & Anna Shuttleworth

STUDENT'S BOOK

NOVELLO PUBLISHING LIMITED
8/9 Frith Street, London W1V 5TZ

Order No: NOV 120343

INTRODUCTION

This book is meant for those beginning to play the cello at any age from ten or eleven upwards. It is not meant for very young children. Its aim is to offer a direct and interesting route to sound technique, with emphasis on good intonation and fluency in the lower positions, ability to cope with straightforward bowings in normal use, and quick reaction to the printed note. Exercises have been kept short (studies in older tutors are usually far too long for the beginner with limited time available); wherever possible, real music has been used, either with piano accompaniment or arranged in duet form, so that the player always has a musical incentive to overcome technical difficulties, and can begin at once to take part in music-making with others.

A good teacher is a necessity, especially in the early stages. We say nothing about playing position or ways of holding the bow, because these things must be demonstrated. Personal variations of physique and the teacher's own preferences also need scope for expression. We don't deal with rudiments of notation; plenty of information on these is available elsewhere: however, musical complexities, such as rests, ties, and dotted notes, have been introduced by gradual stages.

The order in which technical points are taken may not appeal to all teachers. Within limits, this order can be varied. For example: we introduce fourth position early; but since plenty of first position material appears in subsequent sections, you can put off the study of fourth position till you have begun work on slurs, staccato bowings, back and forward extension. By making use of the contents table you should be able to see quickly which pieces are going to meet your particular need.

To help the learner to practise constructively rather than mechanically, methods of approach have been varied. Some sections are presented in question-and-answer form; some call for fingering and bowing by the player. At all points the learner should be encouraged to think for himself. He should invent his own exercises to meet special difficulties; ask himself why he is expected to play a particular piece at a certain stage; write out scales in varied bowings; memorise and transpose pieces. If he thinks he can devise better fingerings and bowings than those given, let him try them—he may well be justified.

There are three parts to this book:

I A broad section dealing with elements of bowing and use of first, third, and fourth fingers: leading to one-octave scales of G,C, and D.

II Concise sections (often linked with a new scale) dealing in detail with specific points of technique, and covering the four lower positions, normal bowings and bowing patterns, and simple double stoppings.

III Takes a rapid look at higher positions (including thumb positions), difficulties of playing in remote keys, and principles of bowing and fingering.

A supplementary book is published containing piano accompaniments to all the pieces in this book apart from the exercises and cello ensemble music.

Traditional tunes are arranged by Hugo Cole, who also added the second part of *Song of a Minnesinger* (No. 12). In all other pieces by named composers, accompaniments are closely derived from originals. It should be stressed that short and sometimes simplified extracts from longer works in the early part of the book are for practice rather than for performance; but later transcriptions may be used as the basis for a concert repertory. The Malcolm Arnold *Duo* was specially composed for this book.

The original instrumentation is specified within square brackets at the end of pieces when necessary; this information is not given in the book of piano accompaniments.

CONTENTS

Titles

Purpose of Piece
[* First position only]

P=With piano accompaniment
D=Duo for 2 Cellos
(one or both parts to be practised)

PART ONE
LAYING THE FOUNDATIONS

			Page
(A) OPEN STRINGS			1
1 Exercise	Repeated notes on open strings		1
2 Exercise	Movement across strings		2
3 Exercise	Mixing note-values		2
4 Heartsease: Traditional	String crossing (three lower strings)	P	2
5 Heartsease: Traditional	String crossing (three upper strings)	P	3
6 March: Purcell	4-string crossing in varied rhythms	P	3
(B) THE LEFT HAND [1, 3, 4]			4
7 Ländler: Schubert	1*	P	5
8 Slow Tune: Cole	1, 3*	P	5
9 Chorale: Bach	1, 3, 4*	P, D	5
10 Hommage: Schubert	1, 3, 4*	P, D	6

PART TWO
BASIC TECHNIQUES

I C MAJOR (two octaves)			7
11 Duet in Canon: Cole	1, 2, 4*	D	7
12 Song of a Minnesinger: N. van Reuenthal	I: 1, 2, 4* II: 1, 2, 3, 4*	D	8
13 Step in, young man: Traditional	I: 1, 2, 4* II: 1, 2, 3, 4*	D	8
14 Gavotta: Handel	C Major: Upper Octave*	P	9
15 Aria Variata: Murschauser	C Major: Lower and Upper Octave*	P	9
II G MAJOR (two octaves) and FOURTH POSITION			10
16 Exercise	Finding Fourth position		10
17 Exercise	1, 3, 4 in Fourth position		10
18 Chorale: Cole	1, 3, 4 in Fourth position	P, D	11
19 La Mère bontemps: French Traditional	1, 3, 4 in Fourth position	D	11
20 Echo Dance: Cole	First position echoed in Fourth	P	12
21 Canon a 3: Cole	1, 2, 3, 4 in Fourth position	Trio	12
22 Dance in quavers: Cole	First and Fourth positions	P	13
23 Ländler: Schubert	First and Fourth positions	P	13
III SLURRED BOWINGS			14
24 Russian tune: Tchaikovsky	Slurs: down bow only*	P	14
25 Christo psallat: Anonymous	Slurs: up and down bow		14
26 There was a pig: Traditional	Quick slurs in 6/8*	D	15
27 Passepieds: Campra	Slurs	P, D	16
28 Irish Song: harmonised by Beethoven	Slurs, dotted notes*	P	17
IV F MAJOR and BACK EXTENSION			18
29 Exercise	Back extension*		18
30 Puisque Robin: Anonymous	Back extension throughout* (one string)	P	19
31 Chorale: Bach	Extended and close positions* (one string)	P, D	19

32	Exercise	Back extension on all strings*		20
33	Ricercar: Ganassi	Back extension on lower strings*	D	20
34	Man in Cellar: German Traditional	First and Fourth positions	P	21
35	Exercise*	⎫ Finger		21
36	Bonny Green*: Traditional	⎭ Exercises		21

V STACCATO — 22

37	Exercise	Staccato on open strings*		22
38	Contretanz: Mozart	Staccato (fingered)*	P, D	22
39	from Concerto Grosso No. 9: Handel	Slurred staccato in one rhythm only*	D	24
40	from Violin Sonata No. 2: Tartini	Slurred staccato in mixed rhythms*	P	24
41	The London Gentlewoman: Traditional	Slurred staccato in 6/4*	D	25
42	Marmotte: Beethoven	Slurred staccato in Fourth position only	P	25

VI D MAJOR and FORWARD EXTENSION — 26

43	Exercise	Forward extension*		26
44	Upon Paul's steeple: Traditional	Scale figures over two octaves*	D	27
45	Gavotte: Handel	D: I Upper Octave; II Lower Octave*	P, D	27
46	Sir E. Noel's delight: Traditional	D: I First and Fourth position; II First	D	28

VII B♭ MAJOR — 29

47	The Crocodile: Traditional	B♭: Lower Octave*	P	29
48	The Carman's Whistle: Byrd	B♭: Lower Octave; slurred staccato*	D	29
49	Exercise	Back extension in Fourth position		30
50	Round: Frère Jacques: French Traditional	(A) In Lower Octave* (B) In Upper Octave	4-pt.	30
51	Lovers' Fears: Schubert	B♭: Upper Octave	P	30

TENOR CLEF — 31

VIII HARMONICS — 31

52	Exercise	Finding harmonics from open strings		31
53	Exercise	Finding harmonics from Fourth position		31
54	Farewell, my joy: Traditional	Harmonics approached from Fourth position	P	32
55	Exercise	Different approaches to harmonics		32

IX A MAJOR — 33

56	Exercise	Forward extension in Fourth position		33
57	O Hangman: Traditional	Forward extension in Fourth position and harmonics	D	33
58	Chorale: Bach	A: I Upper Octave; II Lower Octave	P, D	34
59	from Flute Quartet: Mozart	A Major	P	34

X HALF POSITION — 35

60	Exercise	Finding Half position		35
61	Exercise	In Half position		35
62	Theme: Schubert	Half position linked to First	P	35
63	Exercise	⎫		36
64	The Buffoon: Traditional	⎬ Finger Exercises		36
65	Shepherd's Hey: Traditional	⎭		36

XI E♭ MAJOR — 37

66	All my thanks: arr. Brahms	First and Fourth positions	P	37
67	Ländler: Schubert	I First, Third and Fourth; II First position*	D	37
68	Freemasons' Song: Mozart	I All positions; II First and Second; III First*	Trio	38

v

XII THIRD POSITION			39
69 Exercise	Finding Third position		39
70 Yugoslav Lullaby: Traditional	I, II, in Third position	D	39
71 Exercise	Linking the positions		40
72 Sarabande: Buxtehude	Linking the positions	P	40
73 Exercise	Extended Third position		40
74 La queue, leu! leu! ⎫ French	Extended Third position	D	40
75 Il était une bergère ⎬ Folk	Extended Third position	D	41
76 Il Court, Il Court ⎭ Songs	First and Third positions	P	41
77 from Ninth Symphony: Beethoven	Third and Fourth positions		41
XIII ARPEGGIOS			42
78 Exercise	Writing out arpeggios		42
79 Round; Ah, Poor Bird: Traditional	Major and minor thirds	4-pt.	42
80 Jigg: Eccles	Arpeggios*	P, D	43
81 from String Quartet, Op.54, No.2: Haydn	Arpeggios	P	44
XIV MINOR SCALES			45
82 Exercise	Ascent and Descent in Melodic Minor		45
83 Chorale: Bach	Melodic Minor	P, D	45
84 Air from 'The Fairy Queen': Purcell	I Linking positions, II Minor scale Continuo style	D	46
85 Exercise	Augmented Seconds		47
86 Gavotte: Marais	Harmonic and Melodic Minor scale-forms	P	47
87 *Let Heaven Rejoice: Redford VIBRATO*		P	48
XV SECOND POSITION			48
88 Exercise	Finding extended Second position		48
89 Folk Song: Cole	Extended Second position	D	48
90 The Hardworking Miner: American Traditional	Extended Second position	P, D	49
91 Exercise	Linking First and Second positions		49
92 from String Quartet, Op. 3, No. 2: Haydn	Linking First and Second positions	D	50
93 Exercise	Close Second position		51
94 Folk Song: Norwegian Traditional	Close Second position	D	51
95 Exercise	Linking positions		51
96 The King's Dance: Praetorius	First, Second and Third positions	P, D	52
97 Theme from Rondo: Schubert	First to Fourth positions	P	52
98 *Canon a 2: Bach CHROMATIC SCALES*			53
XVI INTERVAL-PATTERNS			54
99 Exercise	Fingering and Playing Broken Scales		54
100 Ground from 'The Tempest': Purcell	Thirds and Fifths	D	54
101 Variation on a Minuet: Arne	Sixths	D	55
102 Bass from Third Orch. Suite: Bach	Octaves		56
103 *FINGER EXERCISES*			56
XVII CHORDS			57
104 Exercise	One fingered part*		57
105 Duet in three parts: Cole	I One moving part, II Pizzicato chords	D	57
106 All people that on earth: Genevan Psalter	Two-note chords, both parts fingered*	D	58
107 Exercise	Three-note chords*		58
108 Folies D'Espagne: Marais	Interspersed chords, changing positions		58
109 The Earl of Sussex's Delight: Hume	Interspersed chords: I Changing position	Trio	59
	II First position*		59

XVIII BOWING AND FINGERING STUDIES   60

  (A) FOR STRENGTH, SPEED AND CO-ORDINATION

110 Exercise   Simple and Complex Crossings; shifts in sequence   60
111 from Organ Concerto: Handel   Spiccato   D   61
112 from Organ Concerto: Handel   Slurring in triplets   D   62
113 A Double: Pepusch   Mixed slurs and detached bowings   D   63
114 Divisions on the Dargason: Cole   Varied bowings in 6/8 rhythm   P   64

  (B) CROSS-STRING PATTERNS   65
    1 *Two-string patterns*

115 Exercise   One fingered part   65
116 from Cello Suite No. 3: Bach   One fingered part   66
117 from String Quartet, K.464: Mozart   Two fingered parts   P   66
    2 *Three-string patterns*
118 Exercise   Progressive cross-string bowings   67
119 from Cello Suite No. 1: Bach   Two fingered parts   67
120 from Cello Concerto in C: Haydn   Three fingered parts   67
121 Sonata for a Musical Clock: Handel   Irregular string crossings   68

PART THREE

LOOKING AHEAD

XIX HIGHER POSITIONS   69

122 Exercise   Finding Fifth position from Fourth   **5th**   69
123 Exercise   In Fifth position   69
124 Exercise   Linking positions   69
125 Canon: Mozart   Linking positions   D   69
126 Ane Yeir Begins: Scottish Traditional Second, Fourth and Fifth positions   P   70
127 Chorale: Bach   A new fingering of 58   P, D   70
128 Exercise   Finding Sixth from Fourth position   **6th**   70
129 Exercise   In Sixth position   70
130 Exercise   Linking positions   71
131 Minuet from 'Amphitryon': Purcell   Fourth, Fifth and Sixth positions   D   71
132 The Rosegarland: Schubert   Second to Sixth positions   P   72
133 Exercise   Finding Seventh position   **7th**   72
134 Exercise   Linking positions   72
135 Air from 'The Virtuous Wife': Purcell Linking positions   P   72
136 A Palindrome: Cole   Larger shifts   73
137 from Serenade for Strings: Dvorak   First to Seventh positions   P   73

XX (A) THUMB POSITION, (B) OCTAVES, (C) ABOVE SEVENTH POSITION   74

138 Exercise   Tuning fifths and octaves in thumb position   74
139 The First Nowell: Traditional   Octave scale in thumb position   74
140 O, Ponder Well: The Beggar's Opera   Octave scale in thumb position   74
141 Exercise   Double-stopped octaves   75
142 from Arpeggione Sonata: Schubert   Upper registers   P   76

XXI REMOTER KEYS   77

143 Russian Folk Song: arr. Tchaikovsky   Db Major   P   77
144 Consolation No. 1: Liszt   E Major   P   77
145 Prelude: Liadov   Bb Minor   P   78
146 Russian Folk Song: arr. Tchaikovsky   F# Major   P   78

XXII PRINCIPLES OF BOWING AND FINGERING   79

XXIII EXPLORATORY TECHNIQUES   82

147 Nocturne: Krenek   Serialism   P   82
148 Bagatelle No. 1: Bartok   Polytonality   D   83
149 Duo for Two Cellos: Arnold   D   84

Table of Scales and Arpeggios   86

Duets: Where both parts are to be practised, large music-type is used, and the parts are marked I, II. Parts in small type are for accompaniment only (though they may be found useful for sight-reading practice).

A BASS TO HEARTSEASE (2)

Traditional

5 + Piano

7

MARCH TO A BASS

H. Purcell (1659–95)

6 + Piano

String crossing on three upper strings

4-string crossing in varied rhythms

[Remember to keep a straight bow]

[Keyboard]★

★See Introduction

Playing the Cello (Student)

(B) THE LEFT HAND   [1, 3, 4]

POSITION OF HAND IN NORMAL FIRST POSITION

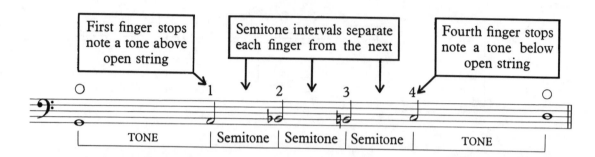

NOTES NOW AVAILABLE ON ALL STRINGS

Using these notes, we can play three scales.

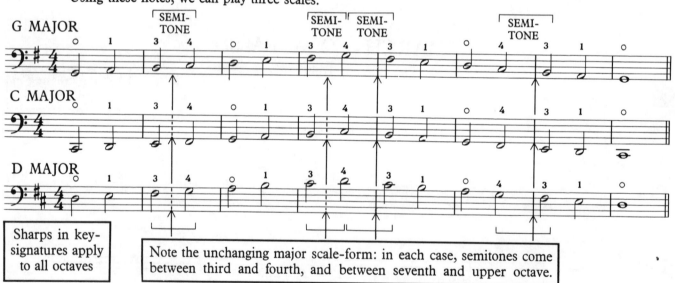

Sharps in key-signatures apply to all octaves

Note the unchanging major scale-form: in each case, semitones come between third and fourth, and between seventh and upper octave.

1 **Sing or hum each scale, to fix the intervals in your mind.**
2 **Find the notes PIZZICATO (plucked).**
3 **Play each scale ARCO (with the bow) using a full bow to each note.**

Work at a scale each time you practise, before going on to the pieces. Each will help the other: by the time you can play a scale smoothly and in tune, you will also be able to play the last piece in this section convincingly.

HOMMAGE AUX BELLES VIENNOISES, D. 734

F. Schubert

10   + Piano   1, 3, 4

[Piano]

For further practice: upper parts of **44, 45; 28** (omit slurs)

As sight-reading strengthens the connection between seeing and doing, so playing 'by ear' strengthens the connection between hearing and doing.

From time to time, practise finding tunes by ear.

The following tunes can all be played with 1, 3 and 4 within the octave scale so far used. Start each on open G or D string.

1 Twinkle, twinkle, little star   2 J'ai du bon tabac   3 I saw three ships   4 Barbara Allen.

Do not go on to the next section till you can play these pieces well in tune and with passably pleasant tone. Good intonation and easy but controlled bowing *must* become habitual at this stage. If necessary, supplement the material given here with easy pieces from other sources.

PART TWO

BASIC TECHNIQUES
I C MAJOR (two octaves)

1

Find notes of upper octave of C Major,
beginning with fourth finger on G string

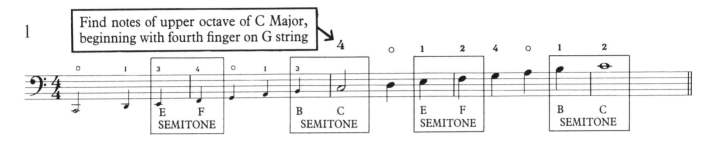

2 TWO OCTAVE SCALE (Practise before the pieces that follow)

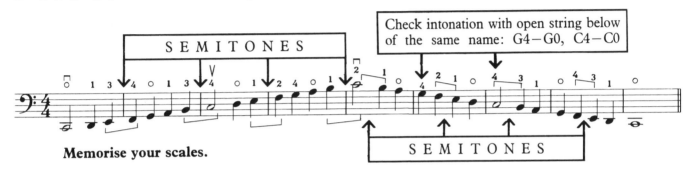

Memorise your scales.

The upper parts of **11**, **12** and **13**, are in the Dorian Mode: the notes used are those of the C major scale, but D is the tonal centre. The lower part of **11** uses the same scale, transposed down a fifth.

11 DUET IN CANON
Hugo Cole

1, 2, 4

Note that second finger
on the G string
gives B♭

SONG OF A MINNESINGER

12

N. van Reuenthal (died c. 1240)

Upper part 1, 2, 4
Lower part 1, 2, 3, 4

STEP IN, YOUNG MAN, I KNOW YOUR FACE

13

Traditional

Upper part 1, 2, 4
Lower part 1, 2, 3, 4

For further practice: **24**, **26** (omitting slurs)

GAVOTTA

14 + Piano

C Major
Upper Octave

DA CAPO
(to beginning)

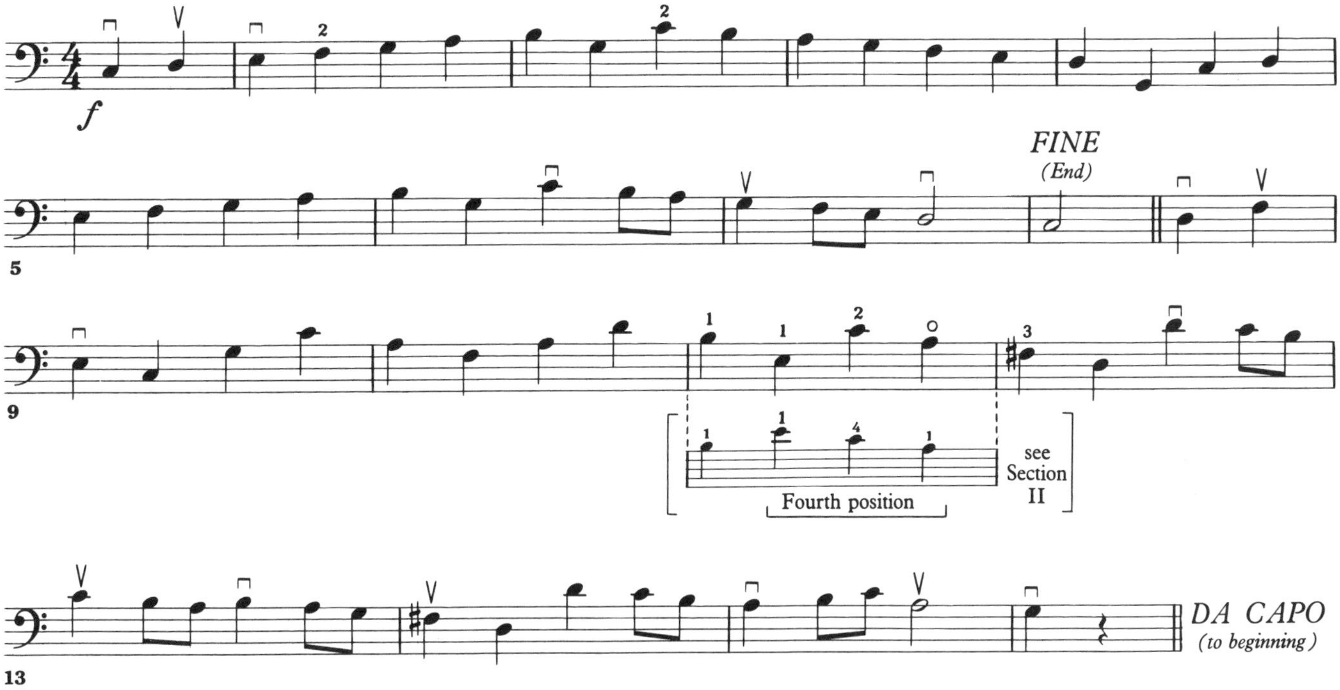

ARIA VARIATA

15 + Piano

F. X. Murschauser (1663–1738)

C Major, Lower
& Upper Octave

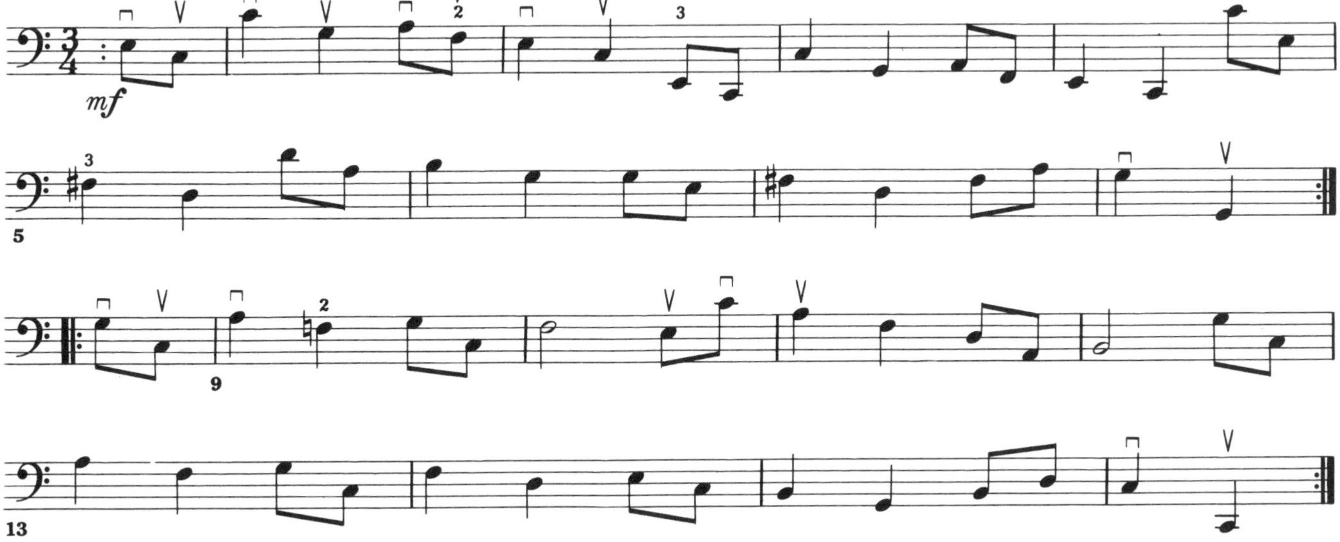

[Keyboard]

After this point, all pieces in First position only are marked with an asterisk *.

II G MAJOR (two octaves) and FOURTH POSITION

18 + Piano

CHORALE
Hugo Cole

1, 3, 4 in
Fourth position

19

19, 20 and 23 are in A minor

LA MÈRE BONTEMPS
French Traditional

ECHO DANCE
Hugo Cole

20 + Piano

First position
echoed in Fourth

21

CANON a 3
Hugo Cole

1, 2, 3, 4 in
Fourth position

This piece is in F Major (see p. 18)

MOVING BETWEEN POSITIONS

Make up your own exercises to practise shifting between First and Fourth positions.

Example:

N.B. 1 Contact between finger and string must be maintained through shift.

2 Hand and forearm must move as one: keep wrist up so that back of forearm
and hand form one level plane.

DANCE IN QUAVERS

22 + Piano

Hugo Cole

First and Fourth
positions

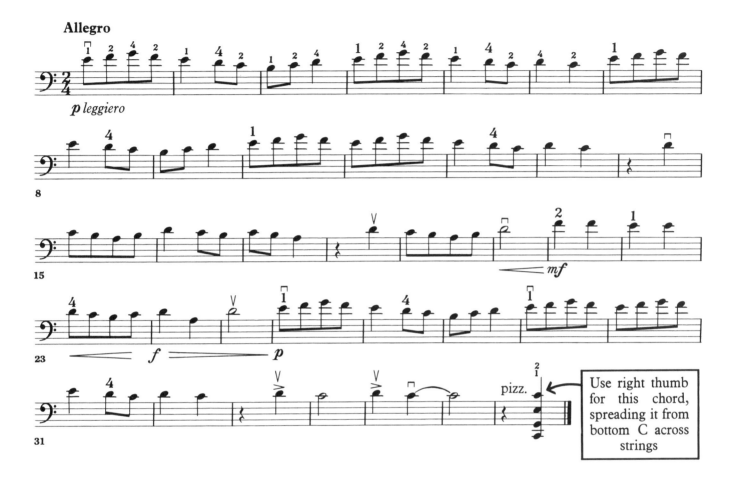

Use right thumb for this chord, spreading it from bottom C across strings

LÄNDLER, D. 366

23 + Piano

F. Schubert

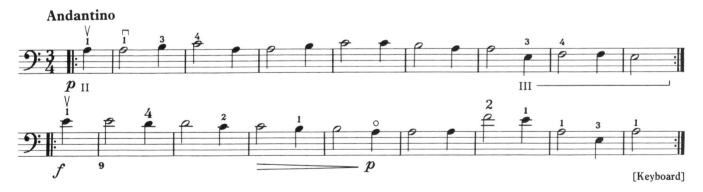

[Keyboard]

	For further practice:	Also refinger and practise:
Fourth position only	42	7
First and Fourth position	14, 25, 27, 34, 35	30, 40

III SLURRED BOWINGS

In legato (smooth) playing, two or more notes may be taken in one bow. Practise the C major scale slurred in pairs.

Count 1-2-3-4

Practise both in First position, and with the top three notes in Fourth position on the D string, as shown below.

Fourth position

RUSSIAN TUNE, Opus 39
P. I. Tchaikovsky (1840—93)

24 + Piano

(First position only) ✱ | Slurs: down bow only

see Ex. 52

[Piano]

CHRISTO PSALLAT
14th century anonymous

25

Slurs: up and down bow

THERE WAS A PIG

26

Traditional

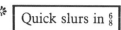

PASSEPIEDS *L'Europe Galante*
A. Campra (1660–1744)

27 + Piano

Slurs: First and Fourth positions

Distinguish slur-mark from tie. Tie indicates that the first note is prolonged without a fresh attack on the second.

IRISH SONG

Harmonised by L. van Beethoven (1770—1827)

The rhythm ♩. ♪♪♩ is introduced for the first time in this piece.
If it gives difficulty, count in quavers:

1 - 2 - 3 - 4 - 5 - 6 - 7 - 8

Moderato

This *3* is not a fingering, but shows a
triplet group (a beat divided into three)

[Voice and Piano Trio]

1, 3, 4, slurs,
dotted notes

[Keyboard]

IV F MAJOR and BACK EXTENSION

The F major scale takes the same fingering as the upper octave of C.

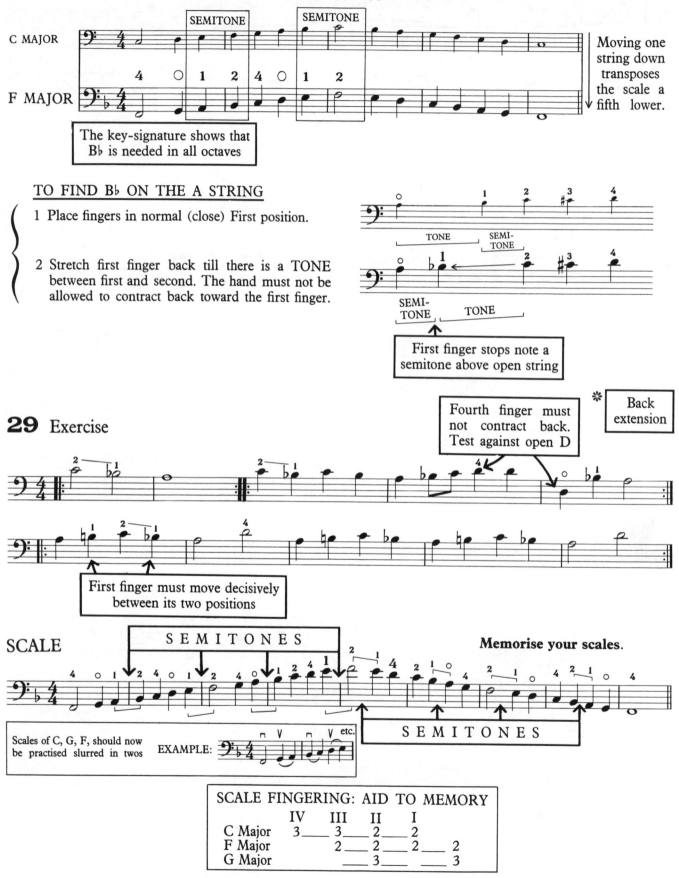

Playing the Cello (Student)

PUISQUE ROBIN J'AY A NOM

Anonymous 15th century

30 + Piano

*Back extension throughout

CHORALE, BWV 386

J. S. Bach

31 + Piano

*First position, extended and close

Accidental B♮ lasts the whole bar

Back extension on G string gives E♭

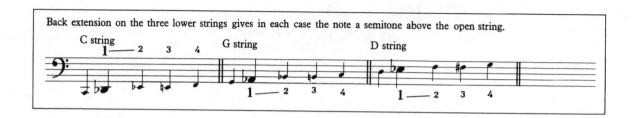

Back extension on the three lower strings gives in each case the note a semitone above the open string.

32 Exercise

* Back extension on all strings

E♮ in close position

A♮ in close position

RICERCAR
Silvestro Ganassi (b. 1492)

33

* First position, back extension on lower strings

[Write in for yourself any fingerings that you need]

Note the use of E flat

Play with firm even tone, and equal pull on both strings

[Viol da Gamba]

MAN IN CELLAR

German Traditional (19th century)
from Fink *Musikalischer Hausschatz*

34 + Piano

First and Fourth positions

★FINGER EXERCISES
35

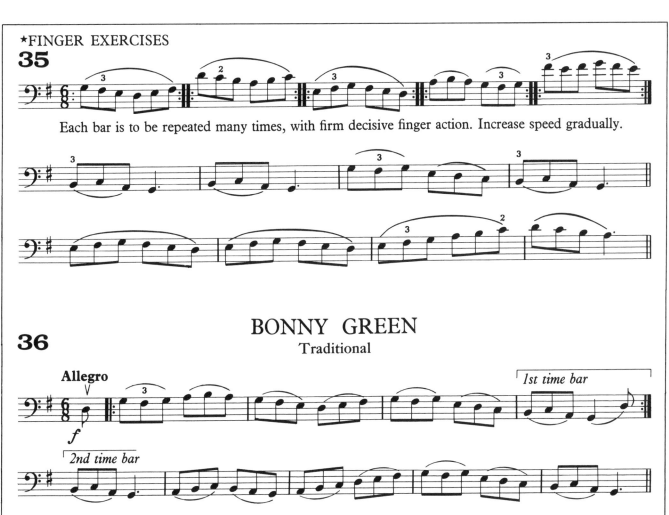

Each bar is to be repeated many times, with firm decisive finger action. Increase speed gradually.

BONNY GREEN

Traditional

36

V STACCATO

Legato bowing, with no gaps at bow changes, produces smooth continuous sounds. To produce sharp discontinuous sounds, separated by silences, staccato bowing is needed.

(but composers leave something to the discretion of the performer: different music passages call for varying degrees of separateness)

PRACTISE STACCATO FIRST IN SLOW MOTION

(a) Place bow on string to make firm contact.

(b) Swiftly release pressure as you begin to play.
Let bow travel over string at an even speed, without pressing.

(c) The next bow-stroke must be prepared equally carefully in the silence before the following note.

It may help you to get the feel of staccato to imagine the firing of an arrow; maximum tension is reached just before release; at the critical moment when arrow (or bow) is started on its course, tension is instantly relaxed.

37 Exercise
PRACTISE SLOWLY

Staccato on open strings

In changing strings, bow must be poised on new string at correct angle before you play

Gaps between notes must be clear at all speeds

Staccato scales should be practised in three ways:

38 + Piano

CONTRETANZ *La fenite*, K. 510
W. A. Mozart (1756—91)

Staccato

Staccato notes must be kept short, so that second and fourth quavers of upper part fall into the silent gaps of the lower.

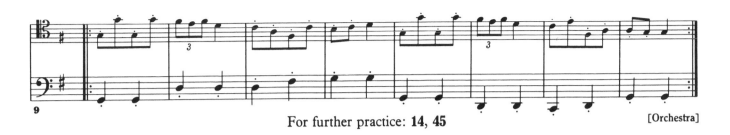

For further practice: **14, 45**

[Orchestra]

SLURRED STACCATO

G. Bizet: Jeux d'enfants

(a)

Play (a) several times, gradually increasing the speed. As the tempo quickens, it becomes more and more difficult to play without overaccenting the short notes or running out of bow. Such passages can be played at speed only by using slurred staccato bowing, in which notes are paired under one bow, but separately articulated.

WRITTEN   PLAYED

(b)

Practise this bowing, *counting aloud* as shown below.

Make sure that clear gaps are left between notes.

SLOW practice is essential.

1 2 Stop 4   1 2 Stop 4   1 2 Stop 4   1 2 Stop 4   1 2 Stop 4   1 2 Stop 4   1 2 Stop 4   1 2 Stop 4

Slurred staccato scales

(a) ... etc.

(b) ... etc.

(c) ...

Note that the rhythm of these three scales is identical: the difference is one of notation only.

Horizontal lines above or below note-heads also imply re-articulation:

39

from CONCERTO GROSSO No. 9
G. F. Handel

Slurred staccato in one rhythm only

40 + Piano

from VIOLIN SONATA No. 2
G. Tartini (1692–1770)

Slurred staccato in mixed rhythms

Music with regular rhythmic patterns often calls for a bowing patterned to match the rhythm, with down bows on strong beats.

41
THE LONGDON GENTLEWOMAN
THE LONDON GENTLEWOMAN
Traditional

Slurred staccato in $\frac{6}{4}$

The slower six-eight of the next piece is easier to play smoothly in slurred staccato.

42 + Piano
MARMOTTE, Opus 52, No. 7
L. van Beethoven

Slurred staccato in Fourth position only

[Voice and Piano]

For further practice: **48**

VI D MAJOR and FORWARD EXTENSION

Lower Octave of D major needs F♯ on C string, C♯ on G string

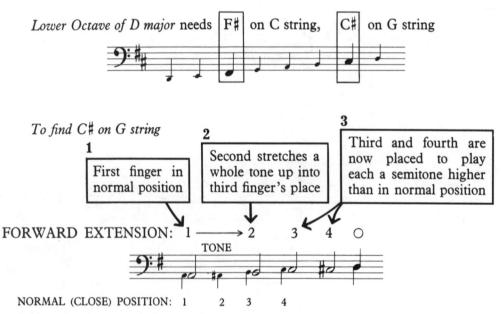

To find C♯ on G string

1 First finger in normal position

2 Second stretches a whole tone up into third finger's place

3 Third and fourth are now placed to play each a semitone higher than in normal position

FORWARD EXTENSION: 1 ──→ 2 3 4 ○

TONE

NORMAL (CLOSE) POSITION: 1 2 3 4

Hand and arm should move freely while first finger remains anchored: for hands too small to hold the position without strain, it may be necessary to walk from finger to finger.

43 Exercise

✱ Extended position

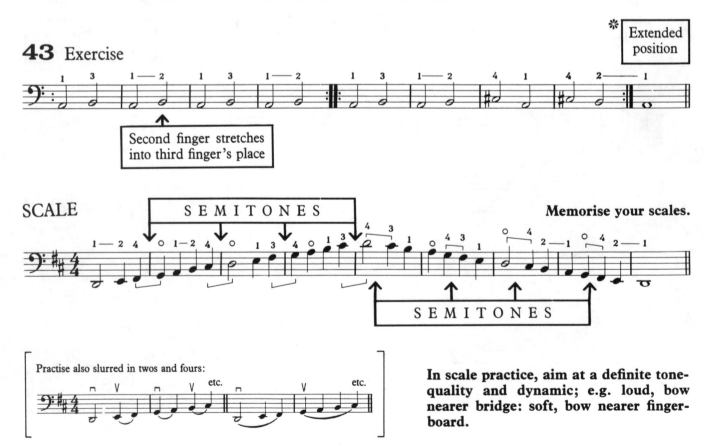

Second finger stretches into third finger's place

SCALE

S E M I T O N E S

Memorise your scales.

S E M I T O N E S

Practise also slurred in twos and fours:

etc.   etc.

In scale practice, aim at a definite tone-quality and dynamic; e.g. loud, bow nearer bridge: soft, bow nearer fingerboard.

UPON PAUL'S STEEPLE STANDS A TREE

44

Traditional

* Scale figures over two octaves

GAVOTTE
from the *Water Music*
G. F. Handel

45 + Piano

* D: I Upper octave
II Lower octave

[Orchestra]

D MAJOR

SIR EDWARD NOEL'S DELIGHT

46

Traditional

D: I First and Fourth position
II First position

VII B♭ MAJOR

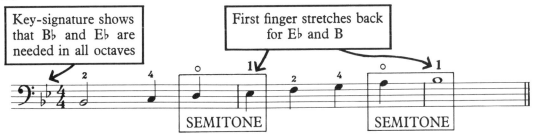

Another bowing for scale practice

At middle or point, using a third of the bow

See page 86 for further bowings.

47 + Piano

THE CROCODILE
Traditional

❋ B♭: Lower Octave

6

48

THE CARMAN'S WHISTLE
W. Byrd (1543–1623)

B♭: Lower Octave
Slurred staccato

UPWARD CONTINUATION OF B♭ SCALE

To find E♭ on the A string

1 Start from close Fourth position.

2 Stretch first finger back till there is a TONE between first and second.

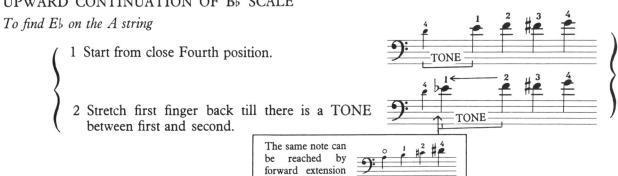

The same note can be reached by forward extension from First position

Playing the Cello (Student)

49 Exercise

> Back extension
> in Fourth position

> Make sure that first finger moves accurately to its new note, a semitone above preceding D

50

ROUND: FRÈRE JACQUES
French Traditional

(A) In Lower Octave

(B) In Upper Octave

> Bb: (A) Lower Octave
> (B) Upper Octave

LOVERS' FEARS, D. 285

51 + Piano

F. Schubert

> Bb: Upper Octave

Smooth, sustained, and concentrated playing is needed.
Every note must sing.

Andante

TENOR CLEF

Higher-lying passages for the cello are often written in the tenor clef, so that too many leger lines can be avoided.

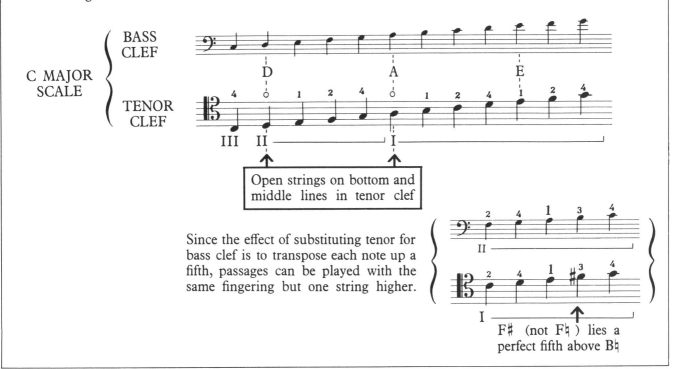

Since the effect of substituting tenor for bass clef is to transpose each note up a fifth, passages can be played with the same fingering but one string higher.

VIII HARMONICS

A string normally vibrates as a single length: by touching it lightly at its midpoint, it can be made to vibrate in two halves, sounding the HARMONIC an octave above its true pitch.

52 Exercise

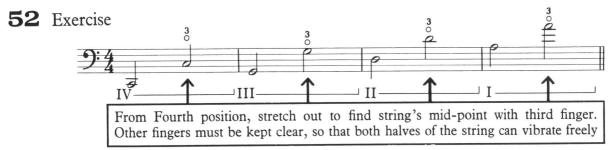

From Fourth position, stretch out to find string's mid-point with third finger. Other fingers must be kept clear, so that both halves of the string can vibrate freely

Finding harmonics from Fourth position

53 Exercise

On returning to a stopped note, leave harmonic free to vibrate till last possible moment

Playing the Cello (Student)

FAREWELL, MY JOY, MY HEART

Traditional

54 + Piano

Harmonics approached
from Fourth position

55 Exercise

Different approaches
to harmonics

Fourth above open
string, lightly touched,
gives two-octave
harmonic

For further practice:
57, 58

Also refinger and practise:
29, 30, 31, 70

IX A MAJOR

Play a scale with the same fingering as the lower octave of D major, but starting one string higher. By moving up a string, you have transposed the scale to a new key, a fifth higher.

D MAJOR

A MAJOR LOWER OCTAVE

FORWARD EXTENSION IN FOURTH POSITION

Extended Fourth position gives   E   F♯   G♯

Upper A can be played as harmonic

Forward extension in Fourth position

56 Exercise

Second finger stretches up a whole tone into third finger's place

57 O HANGMAN, SPARE YOUR HAND

Traditional

Lento

See pp. 39 & 69 for explanation of alternative fingering.

CHORALE, BWV 20
J. S. Bach

58 + Piano

I A: Upper Octave
II A: Lower Octave *

from FLUTE QUARTET, K. 298
W. A. Mozart

59 + Piano

Sometimes it is best to use extended position throughout a passage, even though parts of it lie in normal position.

Con moto   J. Haydn: String Quartet, Opus 10, No. 1

Jump from back-extended first finger to forward-extended fourth finger

See also **45**, lower part

X HALF POSITION

Some passages that lie awkwardly in First position are simpler if the hand shifts back a semitone towards the head:

Half position

First position

First finger stops note a semitone above open string

60 Exercise

Finding Half position

Half position

Half position

Half position

61 Exercise — Finger, then play in Half position

In Half position

(a) H. Purcell: Ground Bass

(b) Oliver Cromwell: Traditional

THEME, D. 823

F. Schubert

62 + Piano

Half position linked to First

Lift bow and start again at heel

Andantino

[Piano Duet]

XI E♭ MAJOR

Using the same fingering as for B♭, but starting one string lower, play E♭ scale.

A new position — Third
Find final D, E♭
on A string

Memorise your scales. See p. 88 for further bowings.

ALL MY THANKS
German Folk Song
Arranged by J. Brahms (1833–1897)

66 + Piano

First and Fourth positions

Con moto

f legato

[1 - 2 - 3 - 4] *p*

cresc. *mf* *p*

67 ## LÄNDLER, D. 145

Practise II first

F. Schubert

I First, Third, Fourth
II First position ❋

Allegro

p

pizz.

Reach A♭ by forward
extension from First position

f

New position (see p. 39)

FINE

mf

D.C.

[Piano]

FREEMASONS' SONG, K. 623

68

W. A. Mozart

Practise III now. (I and II after XV)

I All positions
II First and Second
III First position ✳

[Voices and Instrumental Bass]

XII THIRD POSITION

Passages that are awkward or impossible in First and Fourth positions may lie comfortably under the hand in the intermediate positions. Demonstrate this by playing the extract below in First and Fourth positions; then with the fingering shown.

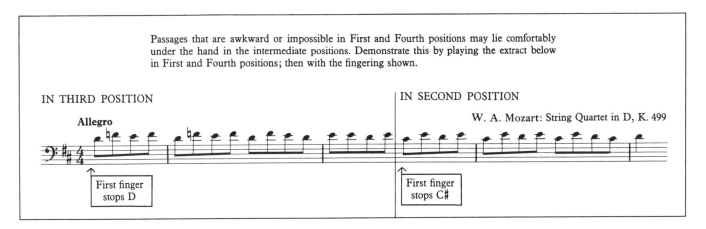

IN THIRD POSITION

IN SECOND POSITION

W. A. Mozart: String Quartet in D, K. 499

(a) CLOSE POSITION

69 Exercise

[↶↗ = check intonation]

Finding Third position

YUGOSLAV LULLABY
Traditional

70

I, II in Third position

THIRD POSITION
[⌢ = match intonation]

71 Exercise

Linking the positions

SARABANDE
D. Buxtehude (1637–1707)

72 + Piano

Linking the positions

Lento

[Keyboard]

(b) EXTENDED POSITION

73 Exercise

Extended Third position

Stretch a TONE between first and second fingers

74

Extended Third position

LA QUEUE, LEU! LEU!
French Folk Song

Allegro

75

IL ÉTAIT UNE BERGÈRE
French Folk Song

76 + Piano

IL COURT, IL COURT
French Folk Song

First and Third positions

77

from NINTH SYMPHONY
L. van Beethoven

Third and Fourth positions

Playing the Cello (Student)

XIII ARPEGGIOS
Major and Minor

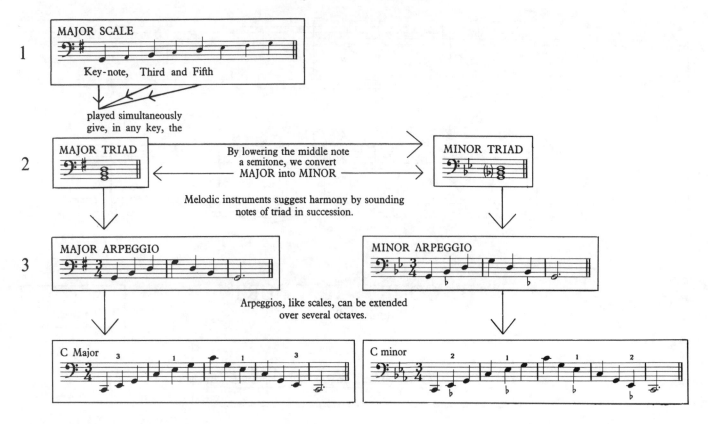

78 Exercise

Write out, finger, and play two octave arpeggios of:

1 D MAJOR

2 D MINOR

AH, POOR BIRD [Round]
Traditional

Think yourself into the major or minor before you play.

1 MAJOR

THIRD defines major

2 MINOR

THIRD defines minor

JIGG
J. Eccles (c. 1650–1735)

 **80** + Piano

 ✻ Arpeggios

from STRING QUARTET, Opus 54, No. 2

J. Haydn (1732–1809)

81 + Piano

This piece will be easier to play after XV, when you can use Second position. It can be attempted in First and Third positions, using the upper fingerings, and omitting small notes.

★[○] = original cello part

XIV MINOR SCALES

(a) MELODIC MINOR

The minor scale differs from the major scale on the same key-note in two important ways:

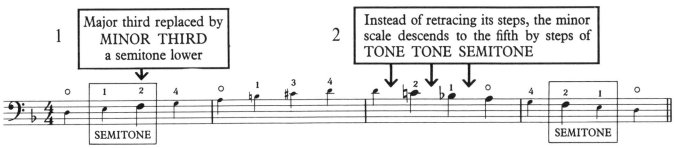

D minor has the same key-signature as F major, and is its relative minor.

Every minor scale has its key-note a tone and a half below that of its relative major.

82 Exercise

Ascent and Descent in Melodic Minor

SCALE OF D MINOR

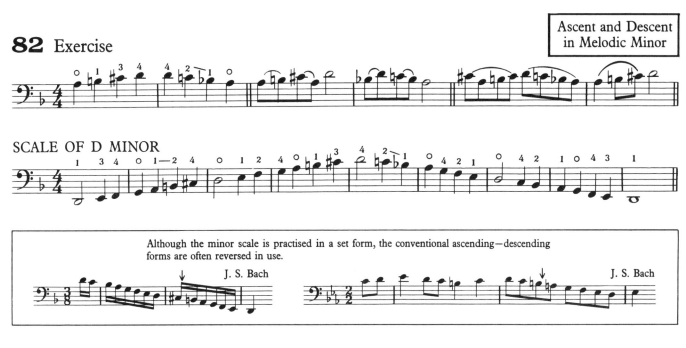

Although the minor scale is practised in a set form, the conventional ascending—descending forms are often reversed in use.

J. S. Bach

J. S. Bach

CHORALE, BWV 405

Melodic Minor

83 + Piano

J. S. Bach

AIR from 'THE FAIRY QUEEN'

84

'I am come to lock all fast'

H. Purcell

I Linking positions see XV
II Minor scale ✳
   Continuo style

In continuo playing, a single cello combines with a keyboard instrument to support a solo voice or instruments. Play the lower part as accompanist, not as soloist. The piano part from a vocal score may be used.

(b) HARMONIC MINOR

Characteristics of the Harmonic Minor scale:

1   Minor third   2   Scale goes up and down by same route.
Between sixth and seventh notes is the big interval of the
AUGMENTED SECOND (three semitones)

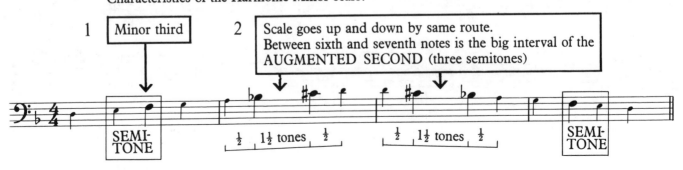

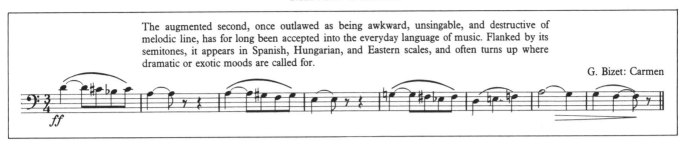

The augmented second, once outlawed as being awkward, unsingable, and destructive of melodic line, has for long been accepted into the everyday language of music. Flanked by its semitones, it appears in Spanish, Hungarian, and Eastern scales, and often turns up where dramatic or exotic moods are called for.

G. Bizet: Carmen

Since Melodic Minor patterns are more commonly met with in string music, Harmonic Minor scales are not set out here for practice. But it is important to recognise the augmented second when you see it, and to remember that it is one and a half tones.

85 Exercise

Augmented Seconds

For hands too small to stretch the big interval, it may be necessary to stretch, then jump to the second note

Fourth finger slides to second note

86 + Piano

from GAVOTTE EN RONDEAU
M. Marais (1656–1728)

Harmonic and Melodic Minor scale forms

Con moto

[Viol da Gamba]

SCALE PRACTICE

1 Revise *and Memorise* all scales learnt so far:
   MAJOR: C, G, F, D, Bb, A, Eb   MINOR: D

2 Practise in varied bowings and rhythms chosen from the table on p. 86.

3 C Minor, G minor, and A minor should be learnt next.
   See p. 88 for fingering.

VIBRATO

Though there is no one way to learn vibrato, all teaching methods would agree on certain essential points:

1. Vibrato must consist of a regular number of even vibrations.

2. The left arm must be positioned so as to allow the hand to move freely and without tension. (Watch a good player to see how hand and forearm are equally involved in vibrato, which is NOT a rolling from the wrist.)

3. Vibrato is used to add to the beauty and intensity of tone. This objective must always be kept in view.

A suggestion for beginners: move the hand (in playing position) up and down the finger-board. Gradually settle second finger in one place, while keeping up movement of hand and forearm.

PRACTISE (a) Long slow notes, counting the number of slow vibrations. Increase the speed of vibration gradually.

          (b) Slow scales with vibrato on each note. Do not stop vibrato when you change finger or position.

LET HEAVEN REJOICE
J. Redford (?–1547)

87 + Piano

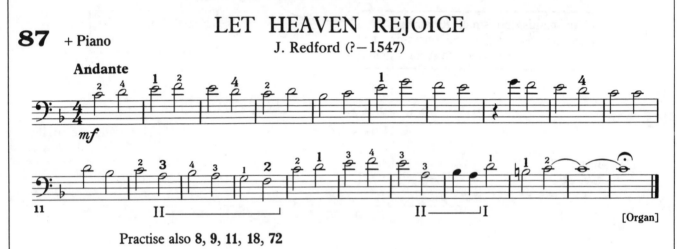

Practise also **8, 9, 11, 18, 72**

As your vibrato becomes better controlled, play through other pieces you have learnt, using vibrato.

XV SECOND POSITION

(a) EXTENDED POSITION

> Finding
> Second position

88 Exercise   [⌣ = match intonation]

89   FOLK SONG
                            Hugo Cole

> Second position

Con moto

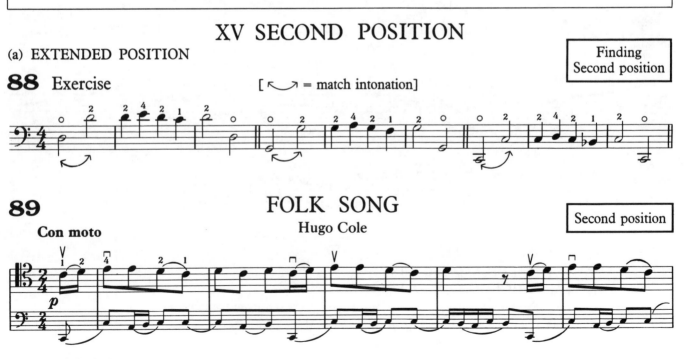

THE HARDWORKING MINER

90 + Piano

American Traditional

Second position

Lento

p

9

LINKING THE POSITIONS

Linking First and
Second positions

91 Exercise

[∿ = match intonation]

Players with large hands
may stretch the fourth

92 ## from STRING QUARTET, Opus 3, No. 2

J. Haydn

Now learn **68 II**

(b) CLOSE POSITION

93 Exercise

N.B. Play over sustained piano chords as shown
(or second cello can sustain the root note of each chord).
LISTEN to your intonation.

1 First finger stops note two tones above open string.

D Major   B Minor   E Minor

Piano plays the key-chord:

2 First finger stops note one and a half tones above open string.

Db Major   Bb Minor   Eb Minor

94

FOLK SONG
Norwegian Traditional

Second position
(Close)

Linking positions

95 Exercise   Remember that a tone is a bigger stretch in Second position than in Third; bigger in Third than in Fourth.

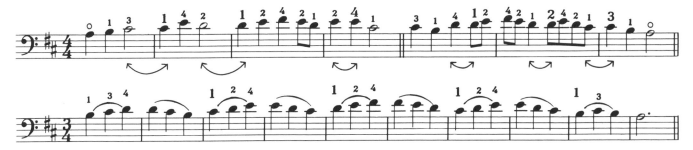

THE KING'S DANCE
M. Praetorius (1571–1621)

96 + Piano

First, Second and Third positions

THEME from RONDO, D. 506
F. Schubert

97 + Piano

First to Fourth positions

[Piano]

Now learn **68** I, **84**, I

For further practice: **51**, **81**, using lower fingerings

CHROMATIC SCALES

A scale consisting entirely of semitones (chromatic scale) is generally fingered with first, second and third fingers only.

Fingering will often vary from this pattern where the scale is used in incomplete form.

F. Schubert: Piano Trio in B♭, D. 898

The note-grouping of a passage may also suggest a different fingering.

L. van Beethoven: Sixth Symphony

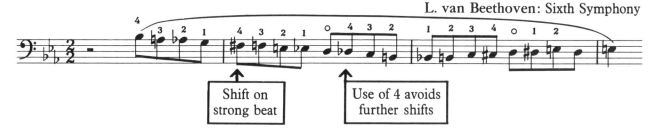

98   CANON a 2 Per tonos, BWV 1079

J. S. Bach

This canon repeats each time a tone higher; write out and play the first repetition in G minor.

XVI INTERVAL-PATTERNS

You can read a sentence at a glance, because you have learnt to recognise words as wholes, instead of spelling them out letter by letter. Music can be read in the same way; not note by note, but by recognising instantly familiar note-groupings.

This section will help you:

      1 To recognise and distinguish intervals.

      2 To translate recognition into action.

99 Exercise

Finger and play scales in broken intervals, first naming the intervals used in each scale.

QUESTIONS

1 Which intervals are always line → line or space → space ?...

2 Which intervals are always line → space or space → line ?...

3 Which interval can be fingered straight across neighbouring strings ?...

4 1 → 4 (on same string or neighbouring strings) gives interval of a ...

5 Why is one interval in (a) shown in smaller notes ?...

6 Why are some intervals in (b) and (c) shown in smaller notes ?...

7 What interval is half the depth of the stave ?...

GROUND from 'THE TEMPEST'

H. Purcell

100

Thirds and Fifths

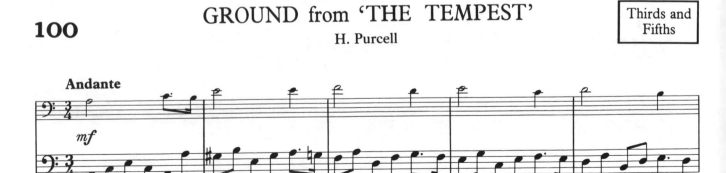

Playing the Cello (Student)

[Strings]

VARIATION ON A MINUET

101 T. Arne (1710–1778)

Sixths

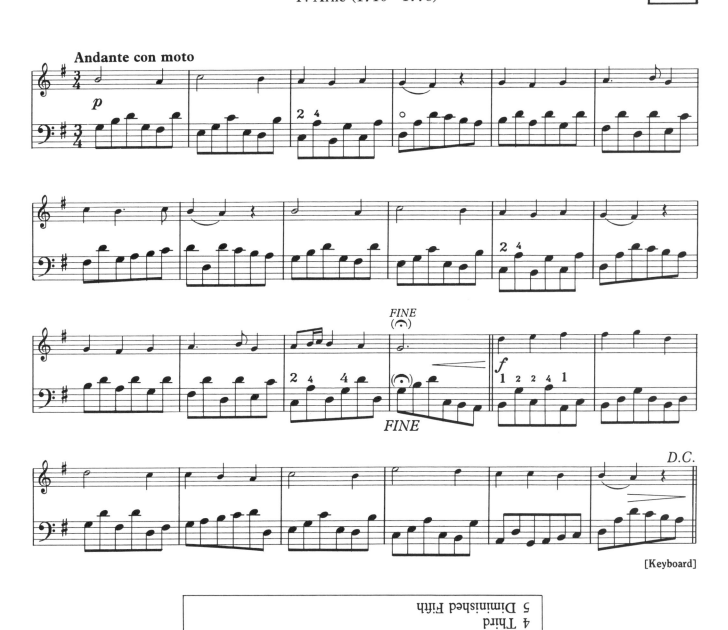

[Keyboard]

102   from THIRD ORCHESTRAL SUITE, BWV 1068

J. S. Bach

Octaves

103   FINGER EXERCISES

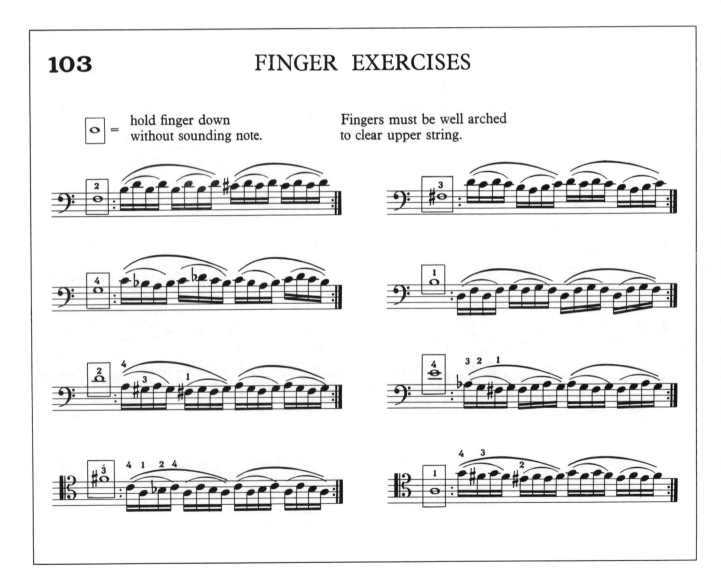

XVII CHORDS

CHORDS ON TWO STRINGS

To produce smooth, well-balanced chords, the bow must be in steady, even, contact with the strings. Both strings must vibrate freely; don't choke the tone by over-pressure.

104 Exercise

✻ One fingered part

The right thumb should control the pivoting movement needed in changing to a new pair of strings

Arch fourth finger to avoid fouling upper string

105

DUET IN THREE PARTS
Hugo Cole

I One moving part
II Pizzicato chords

Andante

CHORDS
ALL PEOPLE THAT ON EARTH DO DWELL
Genevan Psalter, 1551

106

> Two-note chords, both parts fingered

Practise upper and lower voices of double-stopping separately.
If you can memorise the music, you will be freer to concentrate on intonation.

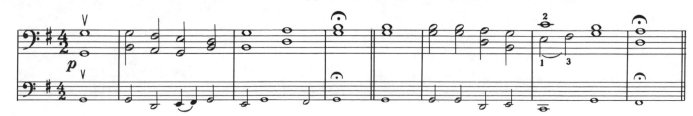

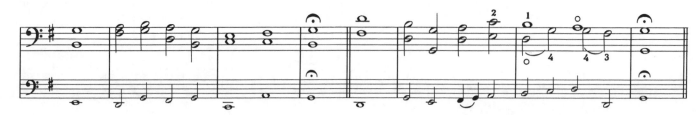

THREE- AND FOUR-NOTE CHORDS

written   played

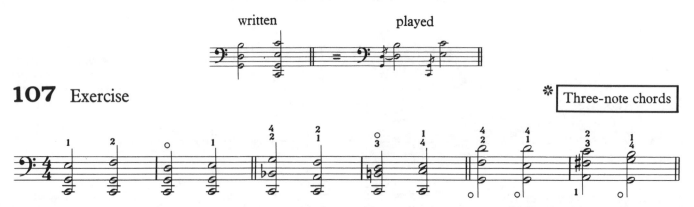

107 Exercise

> Three-note chords

N.B. In playing three- and four-note chords, continuity of tone must be aimed at. The bow must be kept moving on the upper notes for as long as possible before swinging down to the lower string.

TWO COUPLETS
from FOLIES D'ESPAGNE
M. Marais

108

> Interspersed chords, changing positions

Playing the Cello (Student)

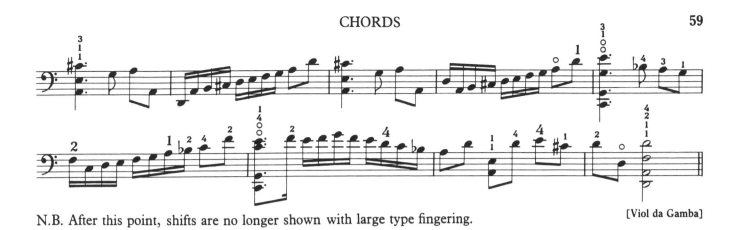

N.B. After this point, shifts are no longer shown with large type fingering.

[Viol da Gamba]

from THE EARL OF SUSSEX'S DELIGHT
Tobias Hume(?–1645)

109

Original for two Lyra Viols and Bass Viol

Interspersed chords:
I   Changing position
II First position✳

⚠️ Scale practice must be maintained.
E major and A♭ major should now be learnt.
See pp. 87 for fingering, 86 for table of bowings.

XVIII BOWING AND FINGERING STUDIES

(A) FOR STRENGTH, SPEED AND CO-ORDINATION

Practise section by section before joining sections to form a continuous whole.

Memorise this exercise.

110 Exercise

Other bowings to be practised. (Decide on your bowing, then keep to it.)

See p. 86 for further bowing patterns.

Spiccato bowing (in which the bow lifts away from the string) must be demonstrated by a good player.

1 At slower speeds: a deliberate lifting of the bow: play near heel.
   (Supple fingers and wrist are needed for good control.)

2 At quicker speeds: the bow is allowed to bounce on the string.

3 The period of rebound must be brought absolutely under control.

PRACTISE (a) In repeated notes on open strings.

(b) Scales with each note repeated four times.

(c) Scales with each note repeated twice.

111 from ORGAN CONCERTO, Set 2, No. 1

G. F. Handel

＊ Spiccato

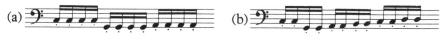

I Quick spiccato: practise ON string first, then spiccato in repeated notes.

(a) ... (b) ...

II Slow spiccato: a deliberate lifting between notes is needed.

from ORGAN CONCERTO, Set 2, No. 1

G. F. Handel

112

Slurring
in triplets

See p. 86 (B) 4 for alternative bowings.

A DOUBLE

J. C. Pepusch (1667–1752)

113

[Keyboard]

DIVISIONS ON THE DARGASON

Hugo Cole

114 + Piano

Varied bowing
in $\frac{6}{8}$ rhythm

(B) CROSS-STRING PATTERNS

Regularly patterned cello parts, usually in accompanying figures, are a normal feature of music from the eighteenth century onwards.

115 Exercise   1 TWO-STRING PATTERNS   One fingered part

from CELLO SUITE No. 3, BWV 1009

J. S. Bach

116

One fingered part

Smooth bowing: bow stays on string at end of each stroke.

from STRING QUARTET, K. 464

W. A. Mozart

117 + Piano

Two fingered parts

Detached bowing: bow should lift slightly at end of each stroke.

2 THREE-STRING PATTERNS

118 Exercise

Patterns based on 4-chord groups.

Practise first by group [1, 2, 3, 4, etc.]; then horizontally [1, 5, 9, etc.]

GROUP A	GROUP B	GROUP C
One moving part	Two moving parts	Three moving parts

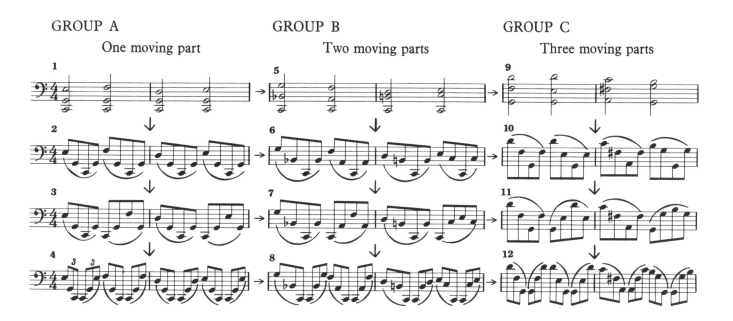

119 from CELLO SUITE No. 1, BWV 1007

J. S. Bach

120 from CELLO CONCERTO in C

J. Haydn

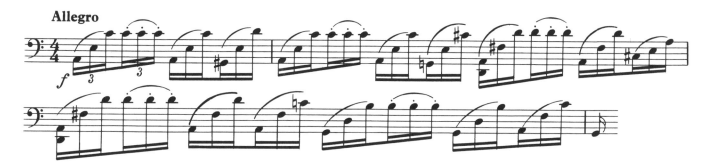

SONATA for a Musical Clock

G. F. Handel

121

Irregular
string crossings

PART THREE
LOOKING AHEAD
XIX HIGHER POSITIONS
FIFTH POSITION

In all positions above Fourth, most players stretch a tone between first and second, and also between second and third fingers.

Finding Fifth position from Fourth

122

Close position

Extended position

123 Exercise

In Fifth position

Extended position

Close position

124 Exercise

Linking positions

CANON
W. A. Mozart (?)

125

semitone

tone

ANE YEIR BEGINS
Scottish Traditional

126 + Piano

Second, Fourth and Fifth positions

A MAJOR SCALE A new fingering

Fifth position

127 A new fingering for **58** [+ Piano]

Play also **57**, using lower fingering; refinger and practise **77**.

SIXTH POSITION

128 Exercise

Finding Sixth from Fourth position

Close position

Extended position

129 Exercise

In Sixth position

130 Exercise

Linking positions

Bb MAJOR SCALE

MINUET from 'AMPHITRYON'

131

H. Purcell

Fourth, Fifth and
Sixth positions

[Strings]

THE ROSEGARLAND, D. 280

132 + Piano

F. Schubert

Second to
Sixth positions

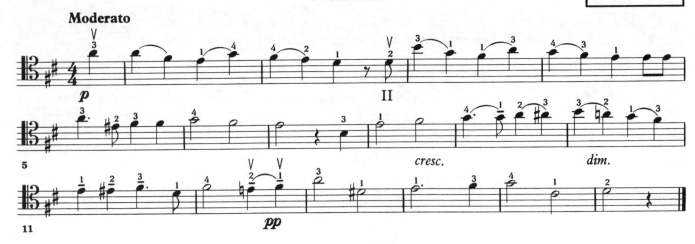

For further practice:

Find the cello part of the second variation of the slow movement from Schubert's D minor Quartet (Death and the Maiden), D. 810, beginning:

133 Exercise

SEVENTH POSITION

Finding
Seventh
position

134 Exercise

Linking positions

AIR from 'THE VIRTUOUS WIFE'

135 + Piano

H. Purcell

136 **A PALINDROME**
Hugo Cole

Larger shifts

Moderato

For systematic practice in shifting, invent exercises based on the interval to be shifted.

Examples:

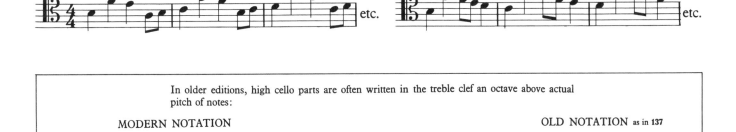

FIFTHS   SIXTHS

etc.   etc.

In older editions, high cello parts are often written in the treble clef an octave above actual pitch of notes:

MODERN NOTATION   or   OLD NOTATION as in 137

=

137 + Piano **from SERENADE FOR STRINGS**
A. Dvorak (1841–1904)

First to Seventh positions

Larghetto

XX (A) THUMB POSITION

The thumb placed straight across two strings at any point should give a perfect fifth.

[If your strings are old or of the wrong gauge, or your instrument is not in good playing order, you may have to tune the interval by adjusting thumb angle.]

138 Exercise   ♀ = THUMB

(a) Tuning Fifths   (b) Tuning Octaves

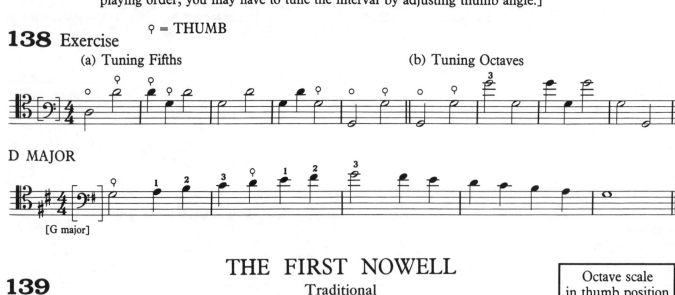

D MAJOR

[G major]

THE FIRST NOWELL

139

Traditional

[Piano accompaniment can be found in some carol books]

Octave scale in thumb position

Play also in C   and E

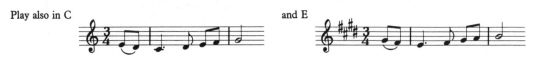

Practise also thumb position scales in C, E and F, with fingering as for D major.

O, PONDER WELL

140

from 'The Beggar's Opera'

Andante

Thumb position can be used to avoid constant shifting in the lower positions.

L. van Beethoven: String Quartet, Opus 135

Fourth finger can be used to extend the scale upwards.

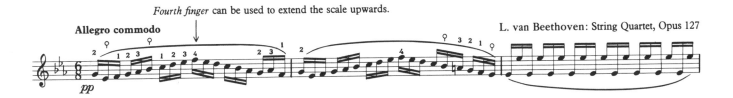

L. van Beethoven: String Quartet, Opus 127

(B) OCTAVES

141 Exercise

J. Haydn: Cello Concerto in D

L. van Beethoven: Cello Sonata, Opus 5, No. 1

(C) ABOVE SEVENTH POSITION

Firm fingering and accurate shifting are more important than ever in the uncharted upper regions: regular practice of three- and four- octave scales and arpeggios is strongly recommended.

N.B. 1 The thumb should lie over the fingerboard, just behind first finger, and ready for action: fluent playing depends on free use of the thumb positions.

L. van Beethoven: Serenade, Opus 8 for String Trio

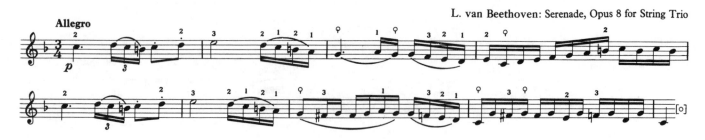

2 Don't confine yourself to ascents on the A string; you should be able to work up and across all four strings with equal confidence.

J. Haydn: String Quartet, Opus 54, No. 1

142 + Piano

from ARPEGGIONE SONATA
F. Schubert

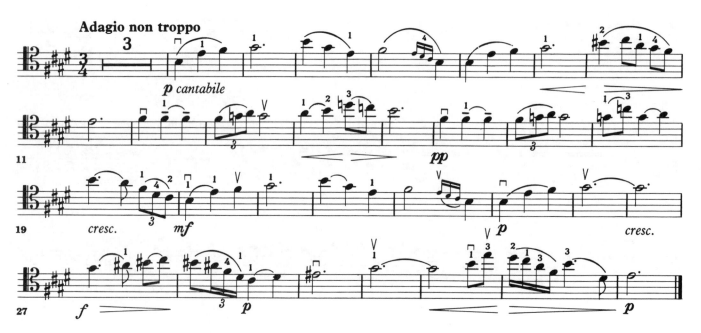

The Arpeggione, now obsolete, was a guitar-shaped instrument, with six strings and frets.

XXI REMOTER KEYS

The technical aim in these pieces should be to move smoothly and freely between positions, maintaining good tone and intonation.

1 Try to anticipate sounds: sing each phrase before you play.
2 Try to fix the sounds of difficult intervals in your head.
3 Try to anticipate the muscular feel of unfamiliar shifts.

RUSSIAN FOLK SONG
Arranged by P. I. Tchaikovsky

143 + Piano

Db Major

[Piano Duet]

CONSOLATION No. 1
F. Liszt (1811–86)

144 + Piano

E Major

[Piano]

PRELUDE, Opus 31, No. 2

A. K. Liadov (1855—1914)

145 + Piano

Bb Minor

RUSSIAN FOLK SONG

Arranged by P. I. Tchaikovsky

146 + Piano

F# Major

[Piano]

[Piano Duet]

XXII PRINCIPLES OF BOWING AND FINGERING

Fingering and bowing are usually left to the player's discretion.

(a) ORIGINAL

Allegro

L. van Beethoven: String Quartet, Opus 59, No. 1

Fingering and bowing chosen must suit the speed and character of the music. It must also allow for your own physique and the present state of your technique.

(b) A SIMPLE FINGERING AND BOWING

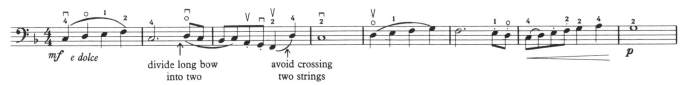

divide long bow into two

avoid crossing two strings

(c) MORE ADVANCED (Many other solutions are, of course, possible)

Unwanted changes of tone-colour and awkward string crossings are avoided by staying on one string.

Suggest bowings and fingerings for the following passages, all from works by Beethoven. The accompanying notes give you a hint as to the nature of each problem.

BOWING

String Quartet, Opus 59, No. 1

Adagio

Bowing and phrasing marks are often not clearly distinguished. Be prepared to use more bow-changes than are shown, remembering the importance of maintaining an even flow of tone.

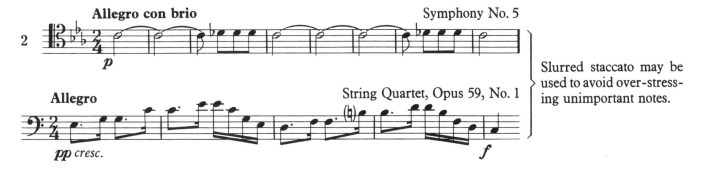

Allegro con brio — Symphony No. 5

Allegro — String Quartet, Opus 59, No. 1

Slurred staccato may be used to avoid over-stressing unimportant notes.

Playing the Cello (Student)

Strong beats or accented notes are usually best taken on a down bow near the heel.

But the ease with which the bow can cross strings at speed must also be considered.

FINGERING

(These passages should also be bowed.)

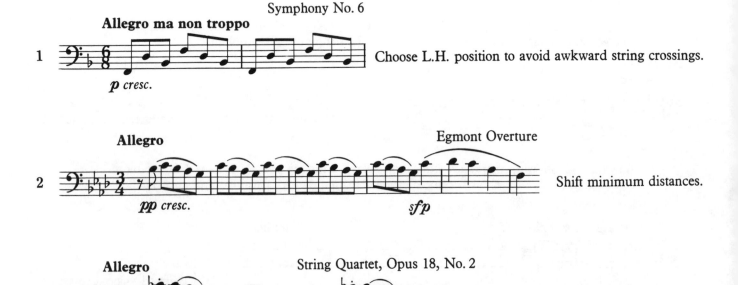

Choose L.H. position to avoid awkward string crossings.

Shift minimum distances.

The place at which you shift can help to establish a rhythmic pattern.

Symphony No. 5

Symphony No. 6

What tone colour is needed for these two passages? It may produce unwanted change of tone-colour to change string: but beware of over-elaborate fingerings leading to insecure intonation. Don't be afraid to make use of the brilliant, open sound of the A string.

Symphony No. 2

String Quartet, Opus 18, No. 2

String Quartet, Opus 59, No. 1

First and second fingers are usually strongest for quick repeated patterns, vibrato on strongly expressive notes, and trills: but third and fourth will often be used of necessity.

String Quartet, Opus 18, No. 4

Adagio molto e mesto

String Quartet, Opus 59, No. 1

It is sometimes useful to stretch a fourth between 1 and 4 if your hand is big enough. Other unorthodox stretches should be used with discretion.

Playing the Cello (Student)

XXIII EXPLORATORY TECHNIQUES

NOCTURNE
from *Eight Piano Pieces*★
Ernst Krenek (1900–)
Arranged by Hugo Cole

147 + Piano

SERIALISM

There is no need to understand the grammar of twelve-tone music to appreciate this piece: but Krenek does, in fact, give an analysis of the compositional methods used in the preface to these 'Eight Piano Pieces'.

★Included by permission of the Composer and Mercury Music Corporation, New York.

BAGATELLE No. 1

148

Bela Bartok (1881–1945)

POLYTONALITY

Included by permission of Editio Musica, Budapest

Playing the Cello (Student)

DUO FOR TWO CELLOS, Opus 85

149

MALCOLM ARNOLD
(1921–)

Playing the Cello (Student)

TABLE OF SCALES AND ARPEGGIOS

Q. Why practise scales and arpeggios?

A. 1 Scales and arpeggios train the hand and fingers in speed, strength, accurate shifting and spacing.

2 They are part of the basic language of Western music.

BE SYSTEMATIC (a) Decide what needs practice.

(b) Choose bowing pattern, speed and dynamic.

(c) *Keep to your choice* till you can do it well.

(A) SEPARATE BOWS

Practise often in long, slow bows for tone production and intonation.

There are many possible ways of practising quicker bowings:

ON STRING	1 at Heel 2 Middle of bow 3 at Point	(a) legato (b) staccato	Beginning ⊓ or V	Fast or Slow	Soft or Loud
OFF STRING	1 at Heel 2 Middle of bow	(a) stroked (b) thrown			

Choose one example from each column:
Example: ON, 1, b, V, Moderato, Loud

Many other bowings can be devised.

MAJOR SCALES Two or three octaves
Practise also downwards.

MAJOR ARPEGGIOS Two octaves

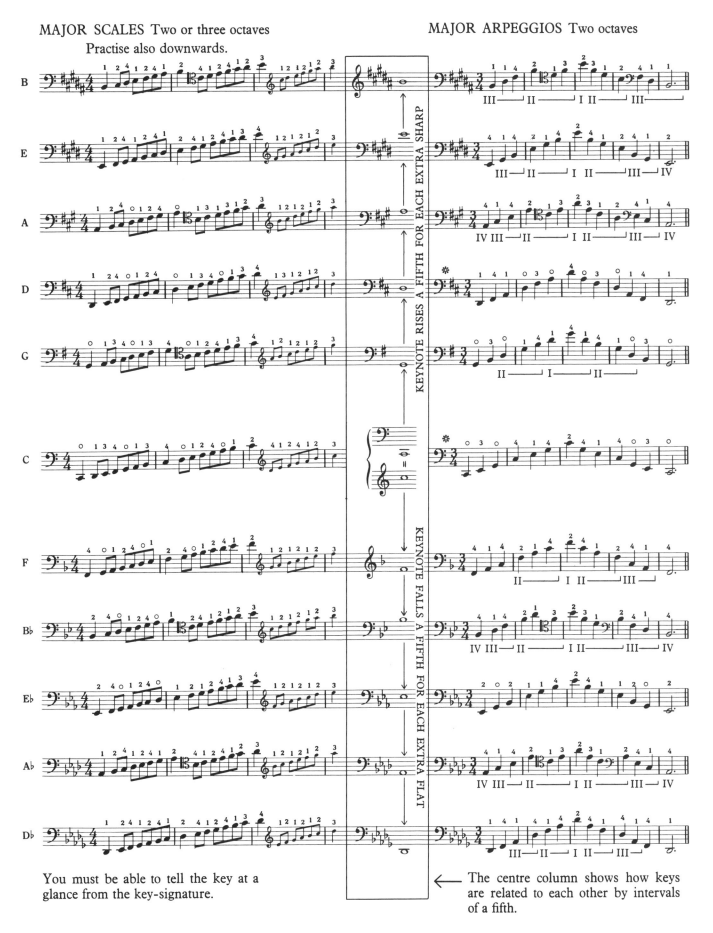

You must be able to tell the key at a glance from the key-signature.

← The centre column shows how keys are related to each other by intervals of a fifth.

MELODIC MINOR SCALES Two or three octaves

HARMONIC MINOR SCALES (see p. 46 for interval pattern). The fingerings given above for Melodic Minor scales will often need adaptation for the Harmonic Minor.

Example:

G♯ Minor

MINOR ARPEGGIOS Two octaves

G♯

C♯

F♯

B

E

A

D

G

C

F

B♭

SYSTEMATIC FINGERING PATTERNS FOR SCALES AND ARPEGGIOS

If only stopped notes are used, unvarying finger patterns can be used in all keys.

TWO-OCTAVE SCALES
In three-note groups

In the third octave, which ascends on one string, an alternative fingering is sometimes used.

[usual fingering: 1 2 1 2 1 2 3]

Scales should also be played up to the top of all four strings using one of these types of fingering.

ARPEGGIOS (Three- and Four-Octave)
In three-note groups

(a) Shifting on key-note

(b) Shifting on third

(c) Shifting on fifth

MAJOR SCALES AND ARPEGGIOS IN SIX SHARPS OR FLATS

Gb scale consists of same notes in another spelling: etc.

DIMINISHED SEVENTH ARPEGGIOS

The diminished seventh arpeggio is made up entirely of minor thirds. It can begin on any note.

Pairs of notes are fingered
1−4 in lower positions, 1−3 in higher positions

Example:

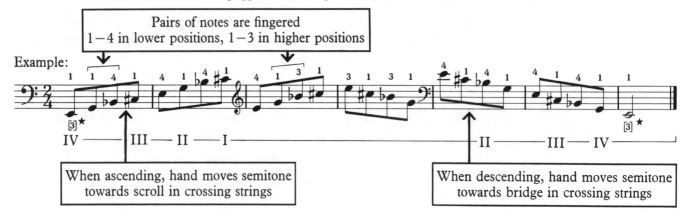

When ascending, hand moves semitone
towards scroll in crossing strings

When descending, hand moves semitone
towards bridge in crossing strings

★The fingering of first and last notes will vary with the arpeggio chosen.
Choose first-note fingering for maximum security of intonation.

DOMINANT SEVENTH ARPEGGIOS

The dominant seventh arpeggio consists of the fifth note of the scale together with the major third, fifth, and minor seventh above this note.

D major arpeggio; compare structure and fingering pattern.

Dominant seventh arpeggio *in the key of G*; this arpeggio always starts on the fifth (dominant).

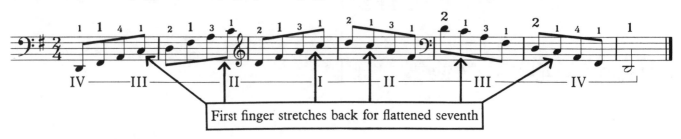

First finger stretches back for flattened seventh

Printed and bound in Great Britain by
Caligraving Limited Thetford Norfolk

10/05 (56512)

MUSIC FOR CELLO

TUTORS & STUDIES

BENOY AND BURROWES
CELLO METHOD
First Year
Second Year
Third Year
SCALES AND ARPEGGIOS

COLE AND SHUTTLEWORTH
PLAYING THE CELLO
Student's Book
Piano Accompaniment

EISENBERG
CELLO PLAYING OF TODAY

SOLO

BENNETT, Richard Rodney
SCENA II

BLAKE, David
SCENES

CHAGRIN, Francis
DEUX PIECES

CONNOLLY, Justin
TESSERAE C

JOSEPHS, Wilfred
SONATA

LEIGHTON, Kenneth
SONATA

McCABE, John
PARTITA

SOHAL, Naresh
SHADES III

CELLO & PIANO

BEETHOVEN, Ludwig van
IRISH SONG

BERGMAN, Erik
QUO VADIS

BLISS, Arthur
CONCERTO
Arranged for cello & piano.

BURROWES, L
SIX EASY PIECES

CAMILLERI, Charles
SONATA

ELGAR, Edward
CONCERTO
Arranged for cello & piano

EVANS, Colin
CELLO TIME
TAKE A CELLO

HARVEY, Jonathan
DIALOGUE AND SONG

HOWELLS, Herbert
FANTASIA FOR CELLO & ORCHESTRA
Arranged for cello & piano

JOUBERT, John
KONTAKION

LEIGHTON, Kenneth
ALLELUIA PASCHA NOSTRUM
CONCERTO
Arranged for cello & piano

MOERAN, E J
IRISH LAMENT
PRELUDE
SONATA

SALLINEN, Aulis
CELLO CONCERTO
Arranged for cello & piano

SAINT-SAENS, Camille
LE CYGNE (The Swan)

SCHUMANN, Robert
INTERMEZZEO

SCHURMANN, Gerard
FANTASIA

SCOTT, Cyril
LULLABY, arranged